Equipped For Ministry

God's Power at Work Within You!

Rudi Louw

Copyright © 2014 by Rudi Louw Publishing

All rights reserved solely by the author. No part of this book may be reproduced in any form *without the permission of the author.*

Most Scripture quotations are taken from the *Revised Standard Version, RSV®.* Copyright © 1983 by Thomas Nelson, Inc.

Some Scripture quotations were taken from the *New King James Version*, NKJV®. Copyright © 1983 by Thomas Nelson, Inc.

All Scripture quotations not taken from the RSV, NKJV and the Mirror Bible are a literal translation of the Scriptures.

The Holy Scriptures are just that, HOLY.

Statements enclosed in brackets were inserted into Scripture quotations to add emphasis or clarify the meaning of what is being said in those scriptures. The integrity of God's Word to man was not compromised in any way. Due care and diligence was cautiously exercised to keep the Word of Truth intact. For example, the apostle Paul said in his second letter to Timothy in Chapter Three, Verse Sixteen that:

"All Scripture is given by inspiration of God (literally God breathed), *and is profitable for doctrine, for reproof, for correction, for instruction **in righteousness...**"* NKJV

Table of Contents

The Marvel of the Holy Bible 5

Acknowledgement 11

Foreword 13

1. I Was Made a Minister 19
2. Not Man's Gospel 25
3. We Impart Wisdom 37
4. A Junction 51
5. Reconciliation is the Message 65
6. The Eyes of our Heart Enlightened 71
7. The Working of God's Might 81
8. God Wants out of the Box! 87
9. God's Reference and Foundation to His power 91
10. Dare to Proclaim the Gospel! 95
11. This Grace Was Given 101

About the Author 113

The Marvel of the Holy Bible

1. Uninterrupted Theme and Inspired Thought

It took *1,500 years* to compile the Holy Bible, involving *more than 40 different authors*. Yet the theme and inspired thought of Scripture continues *uninterrupted* from author to author, from beginning till end.

2. Absence of Mythical Stories

Compare philosophies and theories about creation in the Middle East, Europe, Asia, Africa, and Latin America and you'll find mythical scenarios: gods feuding and cutting up other gods to form the heavens and the earth, etc.

In ancient Greek mythology, the Greeks see Atlas carrying the earth on his shoulders. In India, Hindus believe eight elephants carry the earth on their backs.

But in contrast, Job, the oldest book in the Holy Bible, declares that, *"God suspends the earth on nothing."(Job 26:7)*

This was said millennia before Isaac Newton discovered the invisible laws of gravity that delicately balance every planet and sun in its individual circuit.

Contrary to every other ancient attempt to give a creation account, *the Holy Bible pictures the creation of the earth in a very scientific manner.*

For example, in Genesis Chapter One, the continents are lifted from the seas, then vegetation is formed and later animal life, all reproducing *'according to its own kind',* **thus recognizing the fixed genetic laws.** In addition, we have the bringing forth of man and woman, *all done by God in a dignified and proper manner, without mythological adornments.*

The balance or remainder of the Holy Bible follows suit.

The narratives are **true historical documents**, *faithfully reflecting society and culture* **as history and archaeology would discover them thousands of years later. Not only is the Holy Bible historically accurate, it is also reliable when it deals with scientifically proven subjects.**

It was never intended to be a textbook on history, science, mathematics, or medicine. *However, when its writers touch on these subjects,* **they often state facts that** *scientific advancement would not reveal, or even consider, until thousands of years later.*

While many have doubted the accuracy of the Holy Bible, time and continued research have consistently demonstrated that the Word of God is better informed than its critics.

3. Intactness

Of all the ancient works of substantial size, *the Holy Bible survives intact, against all odds and expectations.*

Compared with other ancient writings, the Holy Bible has more manuscripts as evidence to support it than any ten pieces of classical literature combined!

The plays of William Shakespeare, for instance, were written about four hundred years ago, after the invention of the printing press. Many of his original writings and words have been lost in numerous sections, *yet the Holy Bible's uncanny preservation has weathered thousands of years of wars, contradictions, persecutions, fires and invasions.*

Through the centuries Jewish scribes have preserved the Holy Bible's Old Covenant text, **such as no other manuscripts have ever**

***been preserved*. They kept tabs on every letter, syllable, word and paragraph.** They continued from generation to generation to appoint and train special groups of men within their culture **whose sole duty it was to preserve and transmit these documents <u>with perfect accuracy and fidelity</u>**.

Who ever bothered to count the letters, syllables, or words of Plato, Aristotle, or Seneca for that matter?

When it comes to the New Testament, the actual number of preserved manuscripts is so great that it becomes overwhelming. **There are more than 5,680 Greek manuscripts, more than 10,000 Latin Vulgate manuscripts and at least 9,300 other versions. Further still, there exists an additional 25,000 manuscript copies of portions of the New Testament.** No other document of antiquity even begins to approach such numbers.

The closest in comparison is Homer's <u>Iliad</u>, with only 643 manuscripts. The first complete work of Homer only dates back to the 13th century.

4. Unmatched Accuracy in Predictive Foretelling

The Holy Bible is unmatched in accuracy in predictive foretelling. No other ancient

work succeeds in this, or even begins to attempt this.

Other books such as the Koran, the Book of Mormon, and parts of the Veda claim divine inspiration; *but none of these books contain predictive foretelling.*

This one undeniable fact we know for certain: *While microscopic scrutiny would show up the imperfections, blemishes, and defects of any work of man, <u>it magnifies the beauties and perfection of God</u>. Just as every flower displays in accurate detail the reflection and perfection of beauty, <u>so does the Word of Truth when it is scrutinized</u>.*

Historian Philip Schaff wrote:

"Without money and weapons, Jesus the Christ conquered more millions than Alexander, Caesar, Mohammad, and Napoleon. Without science and learning, He (Jesus the Christ) shed more light on things human and divine than all philosophers and scholars combined. Without the eloquence of schools, He (Jesus the Christ) spoke such words of life as was never spoken before or since and produced effects which lie beyond the reach of orator or poet. Without writing a single line, He (Jesus the Christ) set more pens in motion and furnished themes for more sermons, orations, discussions, learned volumes, works of art, and songs of praise

than the whole army of great men of ancient and modern times combined." (*The Person of Christ*, p33. 1913)

Today, there are literally billions of Bibles in more than 2,000 languages.

Isn't it about time you find out what it really has to say?

Hey listen, the Holy Bible is all about Jesus, the Messiah, the Christ…

…*and everything about Jesus Christ is really about YOU!!*

Study Tips:

Read 2 Corinthians 5:14, 16, 18, 19, and 21.

In the light of these Scriptures, it should be obvious that, if you want to study the Holy Bible, *you should study it in the light of Mankind's redemption!*

Feed daily on **redemption realities** found in the book of Acts, in Romans Chapters One through Eight, and in Ephesians, Colossians, and Galatians. These realities may also be found in 1 Peter Chapter One, 2 Peter Chapter One, James Chapter 1, as well as in 1 and 2 Corinthians.

Acknowledgement

I want to acknowledge and thank one of my mentors in the faith, Francois du Toit, for blessing and impacting my life with the wonderful life changing revelation and conclusion in the truth of the Gospel. *It has proven to be the very tool of God that made me a written epistle, read and known by all men; by it He equipped me and put me in the ministry!*

I borrowed the portion on *"The Marvel of the Holy Bible"* from his website: http://www.MirrorWord.net, as students so often feel they have a right to do with things that come from teachers they respect. Just as Galatians 6:6 says: *"Let him who is taught the Word **share in all good things** with him who teaches."*

Francois: I want to give you the honor, respect, and appreciation you deserve for the indelible mark you left on so many of our lives, and on my life in particular. Had I not heard you preach *on what the ministry is all about and on what it means to be equipped for ministry,* this book never would have been written, *nor would I be living in and ministering from that freedom and fellowship with my*

Father that the truth affords me till this very day.

Thank you, sir!

To all our dear friends and family, for all the love and support, and to Chase Aderhold and all those who helped me with this project:

THANK YOU!

Also, especially to my wife, Carmen;

For keeping me real by being my companion in life and partner in ministry,

I love and appreciate you so very much!

Foreword

Thank you for taking the time to read this book.

Let me start off by saying that *I am totally addicted to my Daddy's love for me.*

I am in love with Jesus Christ, *and that is enough for me!*

The love of God is so much more than a doctrine, a philosophy, or a theory. It is so much more and goes so much deeper than knowledge; it way surpasses knowledge. *We are talking heart language here.*

I write *to impact people's hearts,* to make them see the mysteries that have been hidden in Father God's heart, concerning Christ Jesus, and actually *concerning THEM,* so as to arrest their conscience with it, *that I may introduce them to their original design and to their true selves,* **and present them to themselves perfect in Christ Jesus,** *and set them apart unto Him **in love**,* as a chaste virgin.

We are involved with the biggest romance of the ages. Therefore this book cannot be read as you would a novel: *casually.* It is not a cleverly devised little myth or fable. **It contains revelation and** *truth* **into some**

things you may or may not have considered before.

It is not blasphemy or error though. *It is the TRUTH of God, ultimate TRUTH, and therefore has direct bearing upon YOUR life.* **The Word and the Spirit is my witness** *to the reality of these things!*

Be like the people of Berea the apostle Paul ministered to in Acts 17:11. Open yourself up to study the revelation contained in this book, *to discover for yourself the reality of these things.*

But be forewarned! Do not become guilty of the sins of the Pharisees, **or you to will miss out on the depth of fulfillment God Himself, who is LOVE, wants to give you.**

Jesus said of the Pharisees and Sadducees that they strain out every little gnat BUT swallow whole camels. What He meant by that is that *some people seem to have it all together when it comes to doctrine and they love to argue.* **It makes them feel important, but it is nothing other than EMPTY religious and intellectual pride.** *They know the Scriptures in and out, and YET they are still so IGNORANT about* **REAL TRUTH that is only found in LOVE;** *They are still so ignorant and indifferent* **towards the things that REALLY MATTERS.** They are always arguing over the use of *every little jot and tittle* and over the meaning and interpretation of *every word of Scripture.*

The exact thing they accuse everyone else of doing though, the precise thing they judge everyone else for, *they are actually doing themselves.* That is **they often downright misinterpret and twist what is being said, making a big deal of insignificant things while obscuring or weakening God's real truth; the truth of His LOVE**. They are always majoring on minors **because they do not understand the heart of God and therefore they constantly miss the whole point of the message**.

Paul himself said it so beautifully,

"…the letter kills but **the Spirit BRINGS LIFE***;"*

"…knowledge puffs up, but **LOVE EDIFIES***."*

I say again:

Allow yourself to get caught up in the revelation I am about to share. Open yourself up to study the insight contained in this book, *not only with a desire to gain knowledge, but also with anticipation* **to hear from Father God yourself***;*

…to encounter Him through His Word;

…and to embrace truth, in order to know and believe the LOVE God has for you, *so* *that you may get so caught up in it,* **_that you too may receive from Him LOVES' impartation of LIFE._**

This revelation contains within it the voice and call of LOVE Himself to every human being on the face of this earth. If you take heed to it, it is custom designed and guaranteed to forever alter and enrich your life!

"For I would have you know brethren,

that the gospel

which was preached by me

is not man's gospel,

for I did not receive it

from man,

nor was I taught it,

but it came

to me

through the revelation

of Jesus Christ"

~ Galatians 1:11

Chapter 1

I Was Made a Minister

I want us to start in Philippians 1:6,

*"For I am persuaded that He who began a good work in you will bring it to completion **in the day of Jesus Christ**."*

Some translations read *"at"*, as if Paul was referring to some future event, but it really should be read as *"in"*, because Paul was not referring to some future event when he talked about these things. *He was speaking from the reality of what has become ours in Christ Jesus, because of His successful work of redemption;* **which is the more accurate and proper reference to the term "the day of Jesus Christ".**

I am so grateful that *"***the day of Jesus Christ***" has fully come,* and that we do not have to wait for God to one day, in the sweet bye and bye, *finally bring us to completion.*

We can experience God's working, as well as that completeness Paul is talking about, in the here and now.

I am so thankful that faith is always now, and that **we are complete in Christ Jesus,** just as Paul so boldly declared in Colossians 2:10.

I thank God that all those who see these things *may freely enter in!"*

Let's read Philippians 1:6 again,

"For **I am persuaded** *that He who began a good work in you* **will bring it to completion** *in the day of Jesus Christ."*

Another translation says,

*"***I am confident** *of this very thing, that He who began a good work within you* **is able to bring it to full completion and fruition.***"*

Hallelujah!

*"***I am confident of this very thing!***"*

I believe that every one of us has a desire in our hearts to live in the maximum potential that God has called us to live in and to walk in.

And, Father, we are confident that You are the Alpha and the Omega, *and that You work within us that which is pleasing in Your sight!*

Amen!

The whole purpose of any training program in the Christian faith, in the faith of God, is to impart that faith: to get people to grasp and understand their true identity as saints, that they are not just mere natural human beings, but that they are spirit-beings; the actual children of God, in order that they might enter into true intimate fellowship with God as Father, as Daddy, and so also therefore to see those same individuals, those believers, those saints, equipped for the work of the ministry. If that is not the whole purpose and the focus of your ministry, and of your training program, **then my precious brother or sister, you are missing it!**

And so Paul writes and says in Ephesians 3:7,

"Of this gospel I was made a minister, according to the gift of God's grace which was given me by the working of His power."

*"Of this gospel **I was made a minister**..."*

We are all, every believer on the face of the earth, enrolled in the School of the Spirit, in order to be equipped as saints in our fellowship with God, for the work of the ministry, and Paul says that it is **of *this* gospel, the true gospel of God,** that we are made ministers of.

In other words, *God has given us all a ministry, regardless of what **we think** our ministry is.* **He has already given us a ministry *and He has defined for us what that ministry is*. We are to minister <u>this gospel; the true gospel of God</u>, effectively to others**.

So we want to fully appreciate and fully appropriate <u>this gospel</u>, *the true gospel of God, which God Himself has given us and entrusted us with,* in order to *fully enjoy* its benefits, and *fully live* in the richness of the reality of the gospel of Jesus Christ, *and what that gospel implies for us.*

We also want to effectively communicate <u>this gospel</u> to others, in its full implications!

That is what God, by His Spirit and through His Word is training us to be: **People who understand and enjoy and live in <u>this gospel</u>, the true gospel of God, given to us by God Himself. He is therefore at the same time training us to be effective ministers of <u>that</u> gospel**

...**and so** *that is what we <u>are</u>* **in Christ Jesus;** *what we really truly are!*

But we are that **more and more** *as we get engaged in the truth and life of the gospel; as we get engaged in the life-giving-truth of it!*

Grace and peace are abounding to us more and more, *all the time, as we are increasing in insight and revelation* **in the knowledge and grace of Jesus Christ.**

Paul says, *"I was* **made***…"*

And that word, *"**made**"* in the Greek is the word *'GINOMI',* and it is a very precious word that is found quite often in the Scriptures. It's a word that means *"**to give birth to**"*. In other words, Paul was saying: *"**I was given birth to**…"*

*"This ministry was **birthed** within me…"*

*"…**it was given birth to in me**..."*

*"…**it was birthed in me**..."*

Chapter 2

Not Man's Gospel

This ministry was not something; that Paul said that he received from Man. He says in Galatians 1:10,

"Am I now seeking the favor of men or of God; or am I trying to please men?"

You see, Paul was often in a situation, where his gospel and his ministry of that gospel were depreciated, when compared to the standard of this world. **It was not appreciated, but rather devalued and dismissed; *it was underestimated!*** His gospel and his ministry of that gospel was devalued and depreciated *when measured according to the standard of the wisdom of this world.*

But he says now here in Verse 10,

"Am I now seeking the favor of men or of God; or am I trying to please men?"

He also says somewhere else, he says,

***"I would not be a bond-servant of Christ Jesus** if the applause of Man still moved me, and the praise of Man still mattered to me"*

25

Another translation puts it this way,

*"I would not be **a genuine minister** of Jesus Christ, **if the opinion of man was still important to me.**"*

Paul was **in love with God's opinion,** instead of Man's opinion. He was in love **with God's gospel! He was in love with God! He was in love with Jesus Christ! He was in love with Jesus Christ's work of redemption! He was a love-slave** *to that gospel,* **and to Jesus Christ! That's what his ministry was all about!**

He boldly says,

*"**I would not be** a bond-servant, **a proper minister** of Jesus Christ, **if the opinion and favor of Man still mattered to me.**"*

He says,

"Am I now seeking the favor of men or of God, or am I trying to please men?"

You see, one of the biggest traps the enemy has set for us as the Church, is **to so compromise with the world;** *with the standards of the wisdom of this world,* to the point where we are now not just unconsciously anymore, but *constantly consciously seeking the applause and the favor of the world all the time.*

There are times when we will walk in the favor of the world. We read in the book of Acts that in the early Church, there were times where, because of the impact of the blessing of God, *those people **were in favor with all men**.* But there are other times where that same bunch of people that favored you one day want to crucify you the next, just like they did our Lord Jesus Himself. There were times when the large crowds wept under the anointing and the presence of God as Jesus taught and preached and healed the sick. They felt the presence of Almighty God in His ministry, and yet those very same people turned their backs on Him the next day.

We are not called to live after the standard of Man's applause, amen! We cannot afford to live our lives seeking the favor of Man!

Listen; if you do that in your ministry or in your *"church,"* you may gain a crowd, *but you will never really get anywhere spiritually!*

That doesn't mean that we are out to offend people, *but we are out to please Him, amen!*

We make it our aim to please Him!

God said to Abraham:

*"Walk before **Me** and be ye holy." "Walk before **Me** and not Man,"* amen.

Galatians 1:11,

*"For I would have you know brethren, that the gospel which was preached by me, **is not Man's gospel**..."*

Hey listen, there are many *"gospels"* preached in the world. And oh, those ministers can sound so eloquent, and their message so right, full of beautiful words, wonderful sounding essays, cleverly devised poetry, wonderful little stories, clever little philosophies, wonderfully devised little myths and fables, but they are nothing other than doctrines of men that tickle the ear and impress the ignorant and entertain the minds of the intellectual people. But Paul says,

"I want you to know that there is a big difference between the gospel I preach, and perhaps any other version of it, any other so called "gospel" you may have heard in your past. The gospel that I preach, it's not Man's gospel, it's not the product of the senses..."

Galatians 1:11,

*"...**for I did not receive it from Man, nor was I taught it**..."*

He says in Ephesians 3:7,

*"I was made a minister of **this** gospel, (**the true gospel**) **according to the gift of God's**

***grace**, which was given me **through** the working of His power within me."*

Now listen to me, **you can never excel in ministry beyond the working of His power within you! You can never excel beyond the working of His grace within you! It is impossible!**

Paul says, *"<u>I am what I am</u> **by the grace of God.**"*

His competence, his confidence *is not the product of some man's training,* but it is, and listen now, **according to the working of the power and grace of God in his heart and in his spirit.**

The power of God is measured by the working of His grace within you.

That means, the revelation of grace, the revelation of redemption, of that work of redemption, that work of grace, *fuels the working of God within you, that working* *"...both to will and to do according to the good pleasure of His will."* - Philippians 2:13

Galatians 1:11,

*"…for I did not receive it from Man, nor was I taught it, **but it came** to me **through <u>the revelation of Jesus Christ</u>**."*

The only thing that can equip the saints today is still, *"...**the revelation of Jesus Christ**."*

Peter writes in 1 Peter 1:13,

"Therefore gird up the loins of your minds, be sober, **set your hope fully** *upon the grace,"* (and here is the correct translation from the Greek) *"...set your hope fully upon the grace* **that is being brought to you in the revelation of Jesus Christ.**"

The revelation of Jesus Christ is therefore *the only standard* by which we can measure how sober we are.

There is a lot of preaching and ministry today that is under the influence of human persuasion, clever words, doctrines, and philosophies. But Paul says, "**THIS gospel, the real gospel, God's true gospel**, *this gospel I preach, I did not receive it from Man.* **It came to me**... *It was birthed...* **It was birthed, here deep within me**, **in my heart, in my spirit, through an accurate revelation of Jesus Christ!**"

And Peter writes from the same experience when he said, *"Be sober, gird up your minds, do not yield your mind, your thinking,* **to the influence of any other persuasion, but the persuasion that comes to you through the revelation of Jesus Christ.**" - 1 Peter 1:13

In other words, *"Do not get under the influence of some strong personality **or some strong idea, some strong philosophy that some person is promoting,** but **rather STAY...**"* He says, *"...**rather STAY under the influence of the Spirit of Truth; STAY under the influence of the revelation of Jesus Christ** ...speaking to one another **with the substance of truth,** which the psalms and the hymns and the spiritual songs **inspired by the gospel** contain."* **That's the ministry God wants to birth within us!**

And if you consider yourself to be a part of the Church, or you are considering becoming a part of the body of believers, the family of Christ, *this is exactly what God Himself desires to accomplish in your life.*

You will be disappointed if you come to our church fellowship, or come to us for training, hoping to study the doctrine of this, and to study the history of that, or some other cleverly devised curriculum. I thoroughly believe that God wants to train and equip saints in our midst, and in the Church at large, **through the revealed knowledge of Jesus Christ** that comes through the inspiration of the Holy Spirit, **as He unlocks to your understanding the treasures of His Word of Truth; the gospel of our salvation, the gospel of God!**

So do not look for and expect to receive some little certificate or some little recommendation of Man. That is not what the real *"Church"* of the Lord Jesus Christ is all about. *It was not what either Jesus or Paul was all about.*

So do not look for and expect to receive some little certificate or some little recommendation of Man, **for the Spirit of God wants to equip you and train you in the revelation of God, so you can live in this revelation and know the heart and ways of God, and begin to be the reflection of the impact of His word, of His truth; of His gospel within you.**

Now the enemy knows that he has to do something *to try and limit the effect of the truth of the gospel in your life, to try and neutralize and minimize and cancel the impact of the revelation of Christ in your life.* But he cannot adulterate the Word of God. He cannot do anything against the Truth, contrary to the Truth. But he can affect your spirit. He can affect the environment of your heart and soul. So he comes after you. So I want you to treasure and guard your spirit, to treasure the environment of your heart. Protect that environment on a daily basis and say to God,

"Father God, I will not allow any attitude to interrupt my commitment to You! I will not let anything, any vibe, any feeling, any opinion, any circumstance, ANYTHING, interrupt the environment in my heart. I will keep treasuring Your truth about me in my heart, Your love for me revealed in Jesus Christ!'

Paul constantly had to do the same thing, he had to protect the environment of his heart. In Galatians 1 he says, *"I am not seeking the favor of men..."*

So obviously there was pressure on his ministry. The enemy put pressure on him, people began to seek to put all kinds of conditions around him, but he says,

"I will have you know, brethren, the gospel which was preached by me is not MAN'S gospel;"

"...I did not receive it from Man, neither was I taught it by men;"

"...but it came to me through a revelation (an unveiling) of Jesus Christ;"

"...for you have heard of my former life in Judaism, how I persecuted the Church of God violently, and tried to destroy it..."

He says,

*"I advanced in Judaism beyond many of my own age among my people. That's how extremely zealous I was **for the traditions of my fathers;**"*

*"...**but He** who had set me apart before I was born ...**and had called me and identified me through His grace** ...He was pleased to reveal His son **IN me;**"*

*"…in order that I might **reveal Him** …and **make Him known** …and **proclaim Him** … among **the Gentiles**."* (The Greek literally says:) *"…in order that I might proclaim **Him in the Gentiles**."* (Not just the believers, not the "church" people, not the religious goody-to-shoes …but the Gentiles, **the heathen!!**)

He says,

*"…**When He** who had set me apart before I was born …**and had called me and identified me through His grace** …was pleased to reveal His son **IN me** …in order that I might **reveal Him IN the Gentiles** …**IN the heathen** …when He revealed THIS to me …I did not confer with flesh and blood."*

He says,

*"…**I did not confer with flesh and blood** …in order that I might consider their opinion about it."*

In Matthew 16 Jesus asked the disciples,

"Who do men say that I am?"

Well, they all had their different answers and their little opinions, and philosophies, and different doctrines and teachings. But then He inquired of THEM, His disciples, *"But who do you say that I am?"* And then Peter promptly, boldly, responded, *"You are the Christ, the Son of the Living God!"*

Jesus immediately affirmed Peter in his response, *"…flesh and blood cannot reveal this Peter!"*

"Flesh and blood cannot reveal THIS!"

You see, it's the Spirit of truth; it's the anointing that abides in you that teaches you. It is God Himself who opens your eyes.

You can sit under the most anointed ministry, but unless the truth; that truth revealed in Jesus, that truth about the true identity of the son of man, that Spirit of Truth, that abiding anointing becomes **a reality** in your spirit, *no revelation will break through in your heart!*

1 Corinthians 2:1,

"When I came to you brethren, I did not come to you **proclaiming the mystery of God** *in lofty words of human wisdom. For I decided <u>to know nothing among you</u>* **except Jesus Christ, and Him crucified***."*

That was the beginning of Paul's ministry to them. And I want you to know that *that is always our first approach in bringing the gospel to someone.* Because before someone can enjoy eternal life, abundant life, *they have to be introduced through that veil,* **the torn flesh of Jesus, which exposed to us the love of God in the clearest way possible, and that is what gives us access with confidence into the very presence of God,** *to enjoy all those better things that belong to salvation.*

Paul goes on to say there in 1 Corinthians 2:2,

"I was with you in weakness and in much fear and trembling, and my speech and my message were not in plausible words of Man's wisdom, **but in demonstration of the spirit and of power, so that your faith might not rest in the wisdom of men, but in the power of God.***"*

I am going quickly over these precious rich truths, but I want to enlighten *just a few of them* to your understanding.

Chapter 3

We Impart Wisdom

1 Corinthians 2:6,

"...yet among the mature **we do impart wisdom**..."

Look at those two little words:

"...***impart wisdom***..."

Ephesians 3:7

"*I was made* (GINOMI) *a minister ...by the working of His power.*"

"*...ministry was 'GINOMI...'*

"Ministry was **given birth to** *in me...*"

There is an impartation that needs to happen in order to be equipped. But I want us to see clearly *how that impartation comes, how it happens*.

It says here in 1 Corinthians 2:7,

"*We **impart** a secret and hidden wisdom of God...*"

It is *"secret"* and *"hidden"* because, Verse 9 says,

*"…what **no eye** has seen, **nor ear** heard…"*

You see, flesh and blood cannot communicate this revelation **because it's not available in the physical realm.** Flesh and blood can only communicate within the limits of a sense-knowledge world. Flesh and blood can only communicate the facts that it relates to. It is educated through its environment, through the avenue of its five senses, through sights and sounds, fragrances and tastes, and touch. **But there is another environment that is larger than the dimensions of the physical world …and it is revelation into this dimension,** *it is this education* **that equips the saints for ministry.**

It says here, 1 Corinthians 2:9,

*"…what no eye has seen, nor ear heard, nor the heart of man **conceived**…"*

You see, *"I was **made** (GINOMI)…"*

*"That ministry **was conceived** …it was **birthed** …__within__ me."*

In other words he says,

"My own heart, my own understanding could not conceive this, I could not come up with this on my own; me, in my natural mind, could not

*invent nor receive this **revelation,** which God has prepared for those who love Him..."*

You see, *God has prepared something for this world,* **but He can only communicate it, to those who love Him**.

Verse 10 goes on to say,

"That which God has prepared for those who love Him, **God has revealed to us <u>through the Spirit</u>**. *For the (human) spirit searches everything, even the depth of God."*

Note that it is our spirit that searches out the depths of God. God's Spirit doesn't have to search or research what He already knows, He fully knows the depths of God; *the depths of His heart.* It is our spirit that does not know these things. He, the Spirit of God, the Spirit of Truth, **reveals and imparts and passes this knowledge on to our spirits.**

Verse 11,

"For what person knows a man's thoughts except the spirit of the man which is in Him, **SO ALSO, no one comprehends the thoughts of God except the Spirit of God."**

*"**Now we have received,** not the spirit of the world, but **the Spirit which is from God**..."*

*"...**that we might understand the things bestowed upon us by God**."*

We are going to teach on **these** *"things"*!

"…the **things bestowed upon us by God!"**

2 Peter 1 is also a beautiful chapter defining **these precious spiritual truths** to us, **these things** that are bestowed upon us by God.

Paul continues in 1 Corinthians 2:12,

"We have received the Spirit, not of the world, but of God..."

"… ***so that we might understand*** *the things bestowed upon us by God."*

And now he says, in Verse 13,

*"****We impart THIS****…"*

You see, God's plan with Paul was not just to have one single individual walking with all this volume of revelation, enjoying it all for himself by himself until Jesus comes. **God called him in order to commission him to become a communicator of <u>THIS</u> REVELATION. That was his ministry.**

He says,

"…it's on your behalf..."

That's what '**<u>THE</u> ministry**' is all about. God never did anything for an individual, *just to keep it with that person.* When He touched that woman at the well, **He released and birthed within her a fountain** <u>in order to release that whole town</u>.

'Abraham, count **the stars**,'

'Abraham, **can't you see** for yourself?'

'God has the world in mind with what He is doing in your life!'

I say again saints: **God has the world in mind with what He is doing in the individual's life!** Jesus didn't die for Himself, **He died for the world!**

Now notice this: Verse 13 says,

"We impart **this**..."

Do you see; **it was imparted to Paul!** He says <u>we have been **made** ministers</u>

"...I have been **made** (GINOMI) **a minister**..."

"...**not by Man**..."

"...**but <u>by</u> the revelation of Jesus Christ**" ...**by what is being communicated** <u>**in that revelation!**</u>

He says now,

"...we <u>**impart this**</u> REVELATION..."

41

*"...we communicate **this** REVELATION **so that there can be an <u>impartation</u>, an <u>intertwining</u>,** between <u>the truth</u> of this revelation and the witness in your own heart."*

*"...so that **<u>THIS</u> WORD, <u>THIS</u> REVELATION, <u>THIS</u> TRUTH, <u>THIS</u> GOSPEL can conceive within you, to bring forth ministry pleasing unto God!"***

Notice what He says, he says,

*"We impart THIS **in words...**"*

Words are the vehicles that God uses to communicate His thoughts.

He says,

"No man understands another man's thinking..."

I mean, you can sit there and think anything you like, but I won't know what you think, *until you open your mouth and communicate through the medium of words.*

Listen; until you take those thoughts of yours, *and wrap them up in a word,* and put that word in sound or in picture form, **you cannot communicate your spirit.**

*"How will they believe **unless they hear?**"*
– Romans 10:14

So Paul writes here and he says,

*"We impart **THIS** ...**this wisdom, this truth, this revelation, this gospel** ...**this treasure** ...which God prepared for those who love Him;*

*Oh and what a treasure that is ...**this treasure of redemption** ...**this treasure of being reconciled to God** ...and of **living in Him** ...**this treasure of abundant life in Him**."*

He says,

*"...we impart THIS **in words;**"*

*"...not taught **by human wisdom,** but understood **by revelation!**"*

He says,

*"...**not** taught **by human wisdom**..."*

Because the best human wisdom can offer you is merely the product of the education and experience of a sense-knowledge environment.

Listen, **this** treasure *is not available* to what the eye can see, not even through a microscope or a telescope.

You see, there is a microscopic world that is not available to the natural eye **until you have the right equipment to discover it.** There is an invisible world of sound waves and video waves that make your radio and television work. **It's another world!** There are pictures going through the air right now, *and **we can only tune in to them if we have the right equipment.** But it is still within the realms of the physical world.* You can tap into that world through our modern technology, **but it remains a physical world.**

You cannot tap into **the realm of the Spirit** with your television equipment or your little FM or Satellite Radio, or with your microscope or telescope for that matter. Modern Scientists and nature lovers have been digging into nature for years, and they have discovered little tiny cells and things and they think:

'We have found God.'

But they have only still just found a minute little reflection of the character and person and beauty and love of the Creator.

There is an unseen world not available to the senses of the natural man!

This is where our education systems and Bible Schools have failed us desperately, *because their standard of training **is compromised with the academic standards of this world.*** They have reduced **the greatness of the gospel** *to mere information,* and so they have robbed their students **of its true impact!** Listen to me: It is possible to get stuck in the knowledge realm. It is possible to teach a bunch of doctrines from the Bible, straight out of the Book, *even accurately, but from a natural understanding, sharing mere information,* **and there is no real equipping of saints going on!** Man, I could gold inlay and embroider the certificate, and I could put any kind of expensive robe on you, and put a collar, even the wrong way round or any way round on you, *and still produce a poor excuse for ministry ...a poor excuse for a minister..*

Listen, **nothing** can equip a saint, **nothing** can equip you, **nothing** with work for you, *unless the Spirit of God <u>gets access to your inner being</u>* **and starts transforming your inner life;** *your thinking, your thought life, and your outer life also!* **Only <u>by revelation</u> can the Spirit of God begin to produce in you,** *a capacity to contain the revelation and the very passion of God's eternal purpose for this world;* <u>**the very passion of God Himself**</u>**!**

An equipped saint, a passionate anointed saint, is what God is after *...but it's not available to what the eye can see.* You can focus your little eye lids until you go blind **to try and penetrate that realm of the spirit,** *but it's not available to the casual inquirer, the one whose heart is not wrapped up in God.*

Jesus said in John 14,

"...yet a little while and the world will see Me no more, **but you will see Me.**"

"How will that be Jesus?"

*"…if any man **loves Me** **He will keep** (embrace and treasure) **My Word** (the word of truth; the gospel), and My Father will love him…"*

You see there will be a realization; **a divine feedback!** There will be an **intertwining of the heart; a union,** *born in love!*

It will result in a love affair!

*"…if any man **loves Me** <u>**He will treasure My Gospel**</u>, and **My Father will love on him** … and **I will make My home with him.**"*

"I will come and DWELL and ABIDE <u>within</u> him …and I will <u>**manifest Myself**</u> **to him…"**

Paul says, ***"This is not Man's gospel!"***

You will be disappointed if you come to our group to interact with our ministry *and you want to be trained after the standards of this world.* We don't specialize in that. **But we specialize in God's gospel.**

And let me tell you something: Ministry **is only the fruit produced by the working of His gospel, by the working of His grace in your inner man!**

It is God's gospel, amen! And it is only revelation into *that gospel* **that is equipping**

you in your inner man, equipping you in the spirit, there in your inner man, **to be an able minister of Christ Jesus!**

Hallelujah!

*"...**we impart** this secret and hidden wisdom of God,"*

He says, 1 Corinthians 2:12

"...we have received the Spirit, not of the world, but *of God,* **to understand the things bestowed upon us by God**..."

It's the most dreadful and heartbreaking thing to see a saint walking in ignorance.

Hey Paul says,

"Brother, sister, **we need to understand the things that are bestowed upon us by God!"**

*"...**so that we can appreciate it, and appropriate its affect in our lives!**"*

"...so that we can walk and live and move forward **in the revelation of who we really are as sons of God** *which was revealed in Christ Jesus."*

He says, 1 Corinthians 2:13

*"We impart **THIS** **in words** not taught by human wisdom but **taught by the Spirit!**"*

Now I want to change this translation here. The RSV says, *"...interpreting spiritual truths to those who possess the Spirit..."* BUT the Greek actually says,

"...combining Spirit with spirit."

You see, there are two words for *"understanding"* in the Greek language. The one speaks of mental understanding. It's when I explain something to you that you can relate to through your senses, *and I can convince you with enough evidence that it's the truth,* and thus you can receive an understanding *that measures up to the evidence you have received from your physical environment.* That's how natural persuasion works. It is solely based on the merits of knowledge and understanding; on the merits of an argument that makes sense.

But the Bible also uses another word for *"understanding."* It is the word SUNESI and it literally means **a junction, a flowing together** as of two streams. It is **a junction,** not related to just mental understanding, or to what the eye can see or the ear can hear; to that knowledge, *but it's* **a junction, a flowing together,** *that is related to* **an experience in your spirit, of the working of God's power,** <u>**combining**</u> Spirit with spirit.

You see; there is an **interaction,** *an* **infusion, an interweaving action by the Spirit of God**

within you, where you are literally linked up with God, with His love and with His truth and with His very person.

It is the word 'KAVAH' used in the Hebrew language, in Isaiah 40, where he says,

"…and the young people, the young men even, they will grow weary,"

In other words, *"…they will wear their natural ability out!"* They would reach a point, a place of disappointment *as far as their natural talent and ability is concerned.* You see, in their youth, *they have all that energy and all that ambition, but even they quickly come to the end of themselves.*

But now Isaiah says that,

*"****BUT*** *they that '****KAVAH****' with the Lord; they that encounter* **that experience of the interweaving action of the Spirit of God within them** *...they that encounter* **that experience of the interweaving action of His love and of His truth and of His person; of His anointing within them** *…they shall renew their strength, they shall mount up with wings as eagles, they shall walk and not faint, they shall run and not grow weary!"*

He says, *"...they that '****KAVAH****' with the Lord..."*

I used to think that 'KAVAH,' **waiting upon the Lord**, is something very passive and very neutral and you just kind of hang in there for God knows how long, until God decides to move or do something, or until you grow weary, faint, or fall asleep! But the Bible says, *'KAVAH:'* **they that become <u>intertwined</u> with God.**

"…they shall renew their strength, they shall mount up with wings as eagles do, **they shall <u>run</u> and not be weary**.*"*

Why? *Because suddenly* **God imparts His strength to your spirit; He <u>intertwines</u> Himself with you.** He intertwines Himself with you **through Covenant!** He intertwines Himself **through Covenant knowledge** with natural man.

God imparts to natural man **His ability, His creative ability,** *to restore him to newness of life,* <u>*spirit LIFE*</u>*, a dimension of LIFE that is not restricted to the frustration of the limits of the flesh!*

God adds a new realm of living to Man through the impartation of His Spirit, through the impartation of His love and of His truth and of His Spirit, **through the working of His gospel, through the working of His power in us who believe.**

There can be no impartation of truth, no impartation of LIFE, *until that flowing together is established*.

Chapter 4

A Junction

You see, we need to be released **from any resistance in our hearts and minds** to the true gospel of Jesus Christ. Many sat under the anointed ministry and teachings of Jesus, but their fingers were in their ears! Their hearts became callous to the impact of the truth of the gospel.

I am telling you friend, *guard your heart more than anything else that needs to be guarded! Guard it **so that the sensitivity, the response, the readiness to receive that impartation, that fellowship, that flowing together of LIFE, will not be lost to you!***

That is the only way a flowing forth of the purpose of God can ever be established in anyone's life! That is what that Greek word *'SUNESI,'* **to understand**, is all about. It means **to understand by revelation and from revelation**. It is also the same word used in Matthew 13, where Jesus taught the parable of the seed that was sown.

"And the ones that fell into the good soil are the ones that 'SUNESI...'"

*You see, **that seed became an intertwined reality within them** "…and that seed produced a hundred fold…"*

It was not lost to them! The harvest was not lost to them, the potential of that seed was not lost to them. **They saw its worth and they valued it for the treasure it was** and its harvest was not lost to them *because it **became intertwined with their heart** and their understanding.* God's seed wasn't wasted on them!

This is what Paul was speaking about here in 1 Corinthians 2:13 when He says,

*"We impart **THIS** in words, not taught by human wisdom…"*

In 1 Corinthians 2:4 he says,

"My speech and my message were not in persuasive words of human wisdom…"

You see, it is possible to teach using human wisdom and persuasive words, and certain techniques and methods and ways of saying things, *and to be able to so impact people that you get a set response, a specific created sought after response from people. It's coercion and psychological manipulation!*

But Paul says, *"Listen, why don't I teach that way? Why do I choose not to train you and school you in Homiletics and phonetics and all that, 'how-to-preach-a-sermon,' kind of stuff?'"*

He says I don't teach that way, *"...**so that your faith may not rest in the wisdom and the cleverness of men, BUT <u>rather</u> in the truth and love and POWER of God!**"*

Listen, your faith needs a foundation to relate to! **Don't make it the wrong one!** If your faith and your confidence have a relationship with a human personality, and with human wisdom ...if your faith and confidence is related to that person, and to that wisdom ...if it comes from persuasive word techniques that you have been taught by someone, or that you have learned and picked up somewhere, **you will fail by that faith!**

Oh, I do not deny that through your charismatic personality and through your learned wisdom you may be able to build a large church or ministry and impress all kinds of people in town, or in the whole country and world for that matter, **BUT YOU WILL FAIL! As far as God is concerned, when it comes to gaining real ground in the spirit, in spiritual things, YOU WILL FAIL! YOU WILL FAIL as far as equipping the saints properly is concerned, as far as a genuine flowing forth of true ministry, and as far as a proper flowing forth of the actual purpose and passion of God is concerned!**

See, **God's faith *is of another dimension!* And <u>that faith</u> already has a foundation, <u>*another*</u> *foundation.*** *It is rooted and grounded in the revelation and truth of God's redemption, in the revelation truth and love of God. It is rooted and grounded in, and focused on that truth, on that love, on that revelation of God's redemption,* **and that truth and love gets birthed in your spirit!** There is no other foundation for Bible faith, **for true Christian faith!**

Many people say, *'I'm a believer,'* or *'I'm a Christian,'* or *'I'm a person of faith'* ...but so is the Devil Himself!

But, **true faith, real faith,** is a product of that 'RHEMA' word, of revelation into *that 'LOGOS' made flesh,* **those incarnation and redemption realities.**

I'm talking about the word, *the New Testament Revelation,* **that redemption truth, that gospel of the love of God, which is quickened in your heart and your understanding.**

You see, there is **a junction** there, there is suddenly **an intertwining** in my spirit, and something **leaps within me** called **eternal life; it's *resurrection life!***

I was dead, I was blind. But **now I live! Now I see!** I was lame, **but now I leap, and I run!**

There is **a newness of life** that comes **through the quickening of the Spirit of God that moves upon His word of truth, the gospel of our true origin and of our redemption, and something happens within your spirit.** There is **a communication, an intertwining of truth and of faith and of love**, there is **a covenant established** between God and Man, and Man again comes into a position *where his life gets restored to the radiant image of God's brilliance and His likeness and beauty!*

"...combining Spirit with spirit..."

You see, you are a spirit. Praise God, *we are* **much more** *than what the flesh reveals!* There is much more to us than the size of our muscles, *or even our intellect.* There is much more to us than our social standing, *or even our bank account!* **There is much more to us than our natural birth and family tree can reveal! There is MUCH MORE to us!**

We are eternal spirit-beings, full of eternal destiny! And spirit links with Spirit, and God's gospel, God's Word of Truth is Spirit and life, quickening Spirit life within our spirits. <u>It is the only kind of training worth pursuing</u>!

Listen, I am not interested in *any other kind of seminary or school or education of the mind, we have had enough of that, and gotten nowhere.*

When it comes to ministry, to being equipped for the ministry or equipping others for intimate fellowship with God and for ministry, I am really not interested in any other kind of education EXCEPT the education of the spirit, the quickening of the inner man, the inspiration and activation of the inner man, the Spirit empowerment and releasing of the inner man through revelation, to grow up into the giant image of God here on earth!

You will discover as we continue to study here in this book and maybe if you come to interact with us and sit under out ministry for a while, *that God's plan for you **is more than** just a natural one. It's more than just keeping you alive and existing comfortably here in the flesh on planet earth.* His plan for you *is more than just for your survival* here on this planet ...**while living with a guilt complex and a condemnation complex and a complex of inferiority, and 'I can't make it,' and 'I'm not worth it' and all that.**

In our church fellowship and in our ministry **we specialize in flushing that thing down the drain.**

And hopefully in this book, *you also* **can begin to taste of that freedom!**

When people come to be a part of our ministry, to be equipped by us in our school, I am not interested in getting them to fill out all kinds of little questionnaires, asking them questions like: *'What kind of ministry has God called you to? Oh, and please let your pastor fill out our little recommendation form, or write us a little letter of recommendation about you, just a few paragraphs or so, and you yourself also, please write us a short little essay, and tell us exactly why you are coming.'*

I mean, *'What brought you to this church or this ministry and what position do you hope to hold one day?'* ...and so on and so forth...

Hey listen, I am not interested in your pride and your *'so called' character development* so far, or what you have achieved in the Christian religion up to this point; *what titles and positions of pride and self-exaltation you have held somewhere.* I'm not interested in your ugly old past either, you know, before you turned over a new leaf, and how many mishaps you have had in your life since then, and what your religious ambitions now are, nor even what your own life ambitions for yourself are.

I am only interested in *one thing!*

JESUS CHRIST AND HIM CRUCIFIED!

Christ in you ...resurrection life working in you and through you, the Christ-life fully manifesting in you, **is all I am interested in.**

It's all I am after! *The full purpose of God coming forth in your life,* is all I care about!

I see you as new creatures in Christ Jesus! I refuse to see you in any other light!

Paul says in 2 Corinthians 5:14,

*"**My conclusion in the gospel now compels me**..."*

*"**The love of Christ constrains me; His love now compels me,** to no longer consider **any person** from a human point of view!"*

The last verse of 2 Corinthians Chapter 4 says,

*"...we look **not** at the things that are seen, **but at the unseen realities**,"*

*"...because the things that are seen **are subject to change**,"*

*So the ugly old things that may be hanging around you **are subject to change, as your inner man gets awakened to its true identity, through redemption truth, through insight and revelation into these things.***

Listen, I see a beautiful spirit in you! I see a beautiful potential in your spirit! I see within you the capacity to embrace the fullness of Jesus Christ, and to walk in His fullness, and to then also communicate His fullness effectively!

1 Corinthians 2:13,

*"We impart **THIS** in words, not taught by human wisdom…"*

*"…**not taught by human wisdom!**"*

God sees something in you! God sees something precious in you!

Amen!

And let me tell you, **the biggest release comes when you begin to look at yourself, and then also your fellow Man, *through the eyes of the Father!***

And do you know *what is in His eyes? His heart is in His eyes! And what is in His heart?* A yearning, a burning compassion, which compels Him, *to love this world!*

You see, we've been picturing a God who is ready to judge this world. *But we have never really heard* **the true revelation of the gospel. That is, that He came in person, in the Son, and personally faced our judgment! He revealed that He would much rather face judgment Himself. He would much rather be condemned to hell and die, and let it all come upon Him <u>instead of the world</u>!** *We have never really received THIS revelation in our spirits; THIS impartation, THIS TRUE understanding, THIS FULL understanding* **that He was wounded for our** *transgressions, that He was bruised for our iniquities, that by His crucifixion we are healed!*

No wonder our preaching has been so *filled with death,* **so filled with condemnation and rebuke and guilt and manipulation and beating up on people verbally and spiritually** ...***reinforcing the ministry of death****, the ministry of discouragement, the ministry of the accuser of the brethren, the ministry of Satan,* and *'you're not going to make it, God is judging you!'*

Hey listen; **He faced our judgment in the Son! The Son took our judgment upon Himself and died in our place! I am still speaking law language now, because it seems to be the only language many can comprehend. But the truth is: The Father didn't judge His Son in our place! God didn't kill Him,** *we did!* **We killed the Son of God! We crucified God! And all He ever did was love us even harder!** *"Father, forgive them, they know not what they are doing!" "God demonstrated His own love towards us in that while we were yet hostile towards Him, and didn't understand Him, Christ died for us!"* **He died to demonstrate and prove to us the love God has for us! He died for us because of love! Because He loves us!**

That revelation of Jesus' sacrifice *lives* **in the heart of the Father, and God wants to**

put that heart *in your heart so that your heart is intertwined with Him,* so that your compassion *grows warm and tender with the compassion of God!*

And I am telling you now, that as you begin to grasp THIS revelation, something begins to happen within you **that affect your spiritual eyesight!** *You no longer look at life through the eyes of an ordinary man or an ordinary woman,* **but life takes on new meaning. There is a new challenge to your day!** *Your day is not just another day, where it's off to church, or it's off to work, and this and that and the next thing,* **but there's a new challenge because your life is now redeemed, and so is your time!**

Through the clear demonstration of God's love for you, and your worth and value to Him still in spite of the fall, in spite of your ugly old past ...through that great love with which He loves us, in that sacrifice of Himself, *you have been bought at a price, and so has your time and energy and focus!*

Listen, redeem the time, **make the most of it,** *let redemption have* **its full effect,** *even upon your time; the time spent on this planet.* Let redemption have **its full effect,** so your time can be your servant, **to live to the praise of His glory!**

This is a whole new life that we introduce to Man! Amen! It's not 4 spiritual laws or 5 steps, or this, that, and the other little doctrine or method. **It's a LIFE that we deposit <u>through words</u>!**

Words are Spirit vehicles that impart Spirit truth! They are Spirit vehicles ...these insignificant little words ...just mere words ...seemingly insignificant ...perhaps ...even foolishness to some ...<u>but in themselves containing the very power of God unto salvation, unto wholeness</u> ...containing the very power of God to deliver people, to set them free, to release them from captivity!

Communicating the simplicity of His gospel accurately, effectively, is what God is equipping saints for! ...and not to become better floor washers, carpenters, engineers, scientists, philanthropists, humanitarians, doctors, teachers, professors, judges, politicians, or the next thing. Praise God for those things. They have their place in this world and in society as a whole, and they serve their purpose. *We still have a need for them.* Amen! But those things are natural things and it is not what it's all about. *It's living my life* (in the intimate embrace) *of a reconciled relationship with Father God, and communicating through my life that wonderful fragrance of the knowledge of Him. That's what the work of the ministry is all about: Just living my life in that full intimate embrace of my*

Daddy God, enjoying Him, being in love with Him, and simply allowing that wonderful fragrance it creates in me to get the job done. I'm allowing the wonderful knowledge of Him and the life imparted to my spirit through that knowledge to get the job done ...not the persuasive words of cleverly devised little arguments, and mere intellectual wisdom.

Let the fragrance get the job done!

Let the fragrance of love communicate!

Let that LIFE and that FREEDOM and that JOY communicate!

You see the fragrance is released when that word is spoken; <u>fitly spoken</u>. Because you see, a gracious word, seasoned with the salt of grace, seasoned with the love of God, ready to equip, ready to encourage, ready to edify, creates an environment, an atmosphere.

That knowledge and fragrance of God; that gospel of reconciliation and redemption, that gospel of the love of God for Man, that gospel effectively communicated, accurately communicated, simply communicated from a place of faith, of personal enjoyment, and intimate fellowship with the God in the truth of redemption, creates an atmosphere *that becomes irresistible.*

People may be running, they may be running at their fastest, running away from God, **and suddenly that fragrance hits them!**

Fishers of men! Ha… ha… ha…

And here's that old fish, *just enjoying the world, 'I was just made for this, you know'*

And suddenly that fragrance hits them. The fragrance of the wonderful knowledge of Jesus …*life to life!*

You thought you had it made see, in this miserable old world, but **there's a new dimension of life for you!**

Paul says in 1 Corinthians 2:16,

*"For who has known the mind of the Lord, so that he may be **knitted together with Him**?*

*…**But we <u>HAVE</u> the mind of Christ**"*

Chapter 5

Reconciliation is the Message

Let's go back to Ephesians 3:7,

*"**Of this gospel <u>I was made</u> a minister**, according to the gift of God's grace, which was given me, by the working of His power."*

Ephesians 1:9 says,

*"For He has made known to us, in all wisdom, and spiritual insight, the mystery of His will, **according to His purpose, which He set forth in Christ, as a plan, for the fullness of time, <u>to unite (or reconcile) all things, in Him</u>, things in Heaven and things on earth**"*

Reconciliation is the message of the ministry! Our ministry, God's ministry, the ministry entrusted to us in Christ, that gospel is all about the fact that, God set forth a plan for the fullness of time, in the incarnation, in Christ, <u>to unite (to reconcile) all things in Himself</u>.

All things!

The earth is subject to decay, because of the curse that it's under, the lordship of flesh, the lordship of fallen Man, the lordship of evil. The whole creation yearns with anticipation, with eager expectation *to partake of the glorious liberty of the children of God.*

God has an investment in this world. God sees this world through different eyes. His heart is to be reconciled *with all things on earth, to be reconciled with us;* **to unite us to Him.**

Listen; in Christ, God proved that He is not going to settle for divorce! God's heart is for reconciliation, and for the restoration of all things!

Ephesians 1:9

"For He **has made known to us** *…the mystery of His will …His very purpose* **which He set forth in Christ.***"*

In other words **He has made His heart known to us;** *He has* **revealed it to us. And His heart is all about reconciliation, about our sonship, about intimate fellowship with Him, as Daddy!**

And so therefore, in this book and in our church fellowship, in our gatherings and in our ministry, **we are going to dwell on <u>this</u> revelation, because He has <u>revealed</u> to us, to all Mankind, in Christ***, and therefore in the Scriptures also, in the New Testament teachings of the apostles,* **that which He set forth in Christ in the fullness of time.**

And I am telling you straight, **any teaching program, therefore, that does not emphasize and dwell on <u>this</u> revelation; the revelation of our original righteousness restored to us, is missing it!*

So in this book, and in our church and in our ministry *we are going to keep emphasizing and dwelling on* **that which God set forth in Christ in the fullness of time.** We are going to **dwell** *on the revelation of it.* We are going to **dwell** *on the revelation of righteousness,* **on the Word of Righteousness,** *because it envelopes the total plan of God's redemption!*

To anyone who reads and studies Ephesians 1:9 *it should be obvious to see that* **it's the very basis of Paul's ministry, as well as the very basis of God's ministry** entrusted to the Church.

And so **since it is** *the very basis of all ministry, and for ministry itself,* **my ministry, and your ministry,** *cannot be centered on anything else!*

Ephesians 1:9,

"For He has made known to us, in all wisdom, and spiritual insight, the mystery of His will, ***according to His purpose, which He set forth in Christ, as a plan, for the fullness of time, <u>to unite</u> (or reconcile) <u>all things, in Him</u>****, things in Heaven and things on earth."*

*"For He **has made known to us** …the mystery of His will …His very purpose **which He set forth in Christ.**"*

*In other words **He has made the gospel message known to us**, He has **revealed it to us** so that **we may make it known to the world**, so they also **may indeed be reconciled to God!***

I say again: **<u>this</u> is the total focus of ministry! Therefore our ministry and your ministry cannot be about anything else!**

If God Himself has made <u>this</u> the central theme of all time, and if we as His ministers want to please Him, *we cannot afford to get distracted **and loose the very focus and emphasis of ministry itself!***

We do not dare have any other emphasis and focus in ministry than God Himself!

If you or I **emphasize** and **focus <u>on anything else,</u>** *even if an angel from Heaven shows up with any other emphasis,* **then we are no longer dealing with God's gospel and God's ministry at all. Then we are not busy with the real work of the ministry God has called His Church into! Then we are distracted with little side-line ministries of our own! A little ministry of this, and a little ministry of that! A little prayer and intersession ministry, and a little counseling and inner-healing ministry, and a little deliverance** *ministry, and a little praise and worship or choir ministry, and a little bookstore ministry, and a little bake-sale ministry, etcetera, etcetera, etcetera.*

These modern ministries are not even mentioned anywhere in the New Testament. **They're ministries of our own making! And we are so distracted from the gospel! From enjoying it for ourselves even! We're so distracted from enjoying it, emphasizing it, and making it known to the world! Hey listen; that is what the real work of the ministry is all about!!**

And don't be offended at me now, that's not the way *I* see things, we are dealing with <u>God's emphasis</u>, no mine!

Chapter 6

The Eyes of our Heart Enlightened

Paul continues with His letter, and now I want to bring your attention to what he says down here in Ephesians 1:16,

*"I do not cease **to give thanks <u>for YOU</u>**, remembering you in my prayers…"*

Paul obviously established a connection with a group of people that responded positively to the gospel and became believers of the gospel he preached to them. But now Paul desires to communicate to them that there is *something so deep, **something so precious available to them in this gospel**, through that very same gospel message they already heard from him, **which they cannot afford to miss.***

So he says to them in Ephesians 1:17, *"I pray that the God of our Lord Jesus Christ, the Father of glory, may give you a strong spirit of wisdom and revelation* (or insight) **into the knowledge of Him** (**into His knowledge**)."

Not human wisdom, not the wisdom that comes through the education of the senses,

but a wisdom that comes through the revelation*, through the knowledge **of** Him; **through His knowledge.***

He says in Verse 18,

*"…so that you may have the eyes of your heart **illuminated; enlightened with revelation!**"*

*"…**so that you may KNOW** what is the hope of His calling;"*

In other words,

*"…**so that you may KNOW what He was hoping to achieve in you, and through you, by that call;***

*"…**so that you may KNOW** …the hope to which He has called you!**"*

What is that hope to which He has called us?

In Ephesians 1:5 he says,

*"Through Jesus Christ **He destined us in love to be His children**,"*

*"…according to the purpose of His will … which is: **to unite** (to reconcile) **all things, in Him, in Jesus Christ**"*

He destined us in love to be children of God, restored in every way, in Jesus Christ; restored in a relationship of confidence and

transparency; total innocence, reconnected and in love with God our father, our Daddy! No longer an ugly old heart condition, no longer an ugly old heart *condemning me and making me feel guilty and inferior!*

"...so that you may <u>know</u> ('EPIGNOSKO' in the Greek: **fully know, intimately know**);

"...so that you may <u>know</u> what is the living hope (<u>the reality</u>) to which He has called you..."

Paul says in 1 Corinthians 1:9,

"...He called us into the fellowship <u>of</u> His Son..."

The exact same fellowship, *"the fellowship **OF** the Son".* Not an inferior fellowship, but *'KONONIA',* an **intimate embrace and love affair with God. He has called us to enjoy the intimate embrace of God**, to walk in that *'SUNESI',* that **junction,** that **sweet intimate fellowship**, that **oneness with God**, or *'KAVAH',* that **intertwined covenant love relationship with God!**

That's God's heart for His people!

"...having the eyes of your heart enlightened..."

You see, *the natural eye* in what it sees **cannot appreciate the secret** because, says Paul, *"...The secret was **<u>made known</u>** to me..."*

Or, *"**It was made known so that YOU may know** what is the hope to which He has called us, **YOU INCLUDED!**"*

Paul says,

*"He who has called you **is faithful**…"*

What does faithful mean?

It means that **He is committed to what He has called you to!**

What did God call you for?

And I don't mean, please raise your hands in class and let me know who among you are the evangelists, and who are the prophets and the pastors, and who exactly are the apostles, and perhaps the teachers among you?

This LIFE we are involved in, and the work of the ministry, what we are called into is much greater and larger, *much more precious than what you can define in some functional term.*

Who cares about being anything else *when He Himself has called you into sonship?!*

He called you to 'KONONIA': intimate embrace!

We are co-heirs with Christ, *equal <u>heirs</u>!* Heirs of God Himself! He is our inheritance and our exceedingly great reward!

What we have been called into is so much more precious than mere functional terms!

He called you to <u>be</u> a holy priesthood, <u>a kingly</u> priesthood, to minister unto Him! To minister as unto Him, exclusively, and not unto Man, to try and impress men with titles and positions and the like!

He has called us to minister unto Him. *Our whole ministry is unto Him. The work of the ministry is as unto Him, amen!*

So that He can enjoy **the fruit of the labor of His soul** *...so that He may see in your heart* **a readiness to respond to Him <u>in love,</u> in total abandonment** *...so that He may hear you say to Him,* **from your heart***, 'Lord I am Yours!* **I am exclusively Yours!** *I cannot be bought! Lord,* **I am not for sale, and my ministry is not for sale!** *...And Lord,* **I will not cheapen myself and I will not cheapen Your precious ministry, by looking for titles or recognition from men, not even the sought after title of apostle! Lord I am yours exclusively!'**

You see, *that's where your ministry starts,* **ministering unto Him. <u>And out of the overflow of that communion with God</u>** *He wants to touch your brother,* He wants to touch your neighbor; *He wants to touch the world!*

That's the work of the ministry, *that's what ministry is all about!* That's God's training *program for His church; what His training program is all about, for you and me!*

He wants to train us and equip us and counsel us from on high, from out of that Spirit dimension, out of that spirit and truth reality, *with His eyes of love upon us, and with our eyes of love gazing into His.* *Not with a bit and a bridle, amen! Obligation cannot touch this!*

With His eyes of love upon us, **face to face***, He wants to counsel us and instruct us out of His knowledge,* **seeing eye to eye***, so that* **in the reflection** *of His eye* **there is a communion,** *there is* **an understanding***, there is* **an intertwining, and I am able to <u>walk</u> in the counsel of His will!**

"...having the eyes of your heart enlightened,"

You see, Jesus said that, *"Where your treasure is,* **there will your heart be!"**

Or, **"Wherever your heart and your passion lies, that is what your treasure is; that is what you treasure!"**

The eyes of our hearts have been darkened, **even in the Church, through deception, for many years now! The ambitions in our hearts have been the fruit of deception! It's been birthed by a counterfeit love called selfishness and it has caused a callousness in our inner man! So that we** *could no longer appreciate the purpose of God for His creation and therefore for His Church! And we could only appreciate our own ambitions! And we could only appreciate our selfish greed!*

Whatever focus you have other than focusing on the gospel, <u>becomes your source of frustration</u> as a Christian.

But listen, *God comes* **to quicken our stony hearts,** **to quicken the eyes of our hearts with new vision, a new focus, a new singular ambition!**

Listen, Eli's vision has grown dim! The Church no longer sees, *because its heart is no longer in its eye, in its focus!*

Oh, GOD SAYS,

"You cannot mock me with your songs of praise in your mouth, not even with your revival songs on your lips, while your hearts are far away from Me, and we still do not see eye to eye!"

God picks up the distance easily, *instantly!*

Listen, if there is a distance *in your fellowship with God, in your agreement with God,* GOD SAYS,

"Don't mock me with cold love!"

"I commend you for this and that and the next thing, BUT I have this against you: you have forsaken Me, your first love!"

God cannot be fellowshipped with by a *counterfeit love!* The man-made Christian religion that has taken God's Church captive *cannot please God. Religion cannot please God, no matter how high the praise or how long the prayers!*

Nothing can fellowship with the Father but faith, pure faith, His faith, revealed in Christ Jesus!

Nothing can fellowship with God, but the perfection of redemption, that reflection upon the work of His grace, in your heart ...and the reflection, the radiance, the exhibition and display of the working of that grace, of His grace, in you, within your heart, from within you, in your life!

There is no substitute!

True worship is your spirit fully engaged in God's Spirit, *fully engaged in the Spirit of Truth, and exhibiting that Truth, addicted to it, caught up in it, caught up in God's Eternal Work of Redemption, God's Eternal Redemption Truth!* Addicted to God's Spirit, caught up in Him, with your spirit fully engaged in God, in His love and His Truth, and all that on display in you; God on display in you! That's what God lives

for! True worship is what He lives for! *The working of His grace in our hearts, the working of that Word of His Grace in our hearts, the working of His love in our hearts so that, in Him, we can live and move and have our being!*

*"...**the eyes of your hearts being enlightened**..."*

Through the Spirit of wisdom, through revelation and insight into the knowledge of Him, our eyes become enlightened ...the eye, **the lamp** of the body, **enlightened** ...the <u>lamp of the body</u> **enlightened! God wants to illuminate your world *through the light that He deposits in your heart!***

Ephesians 1:18,

"...having the eyes of your heart enlightened,"

*"...to know the hope to which He has called you, **and to know what are the riches of His glorious inheritance in the saints**."*

*"...**the riches of His glory**..."*

You see, when this revelation breaks through in the Church, *in the hearts of God's people, in the hearts of the real Church,* **they can no longer live in spiritual poverty, in poverty of any kind!** They can no longer live in defeat! They can no longer live under a cloud of condemnation, nor *under a yoke of sin* *either! Because of the glorious liberty of our inheritance, which has become our rich treasure!*

It is a treasure that we no longer place an inferior value upon, and measure by the terms of this world! We no longer measure it by the terms of this world!

It is a treasure no longer limited by deception, but it is a treasure that is the very fruit of the revelation, the fruit of the measure of the gift of Christ!

This treasure that we value above all else is the fruit of the height, the length, the depth; the overwhelming abundance of the love of God revealed in Christ!

Chapter 7

The Working of God's Might

Now Paul says in Ephesians 1:19-21, that **the fruit of the revelation of the knowledge of Him will bring <u>to your understanding</u>**...

"...***the immeasurable greatness of His power in us*** (at work in us) ***who believe;***"

"...***according to the working of His great might***"

"...***the same might which He also worked in Christ*** when He raised Him from the dead and seated Him at His right hand in the heavenly dimension;"

"...***far above all rule and authority, power, might or dominion, and also every name or title that can be given,*** not only in this present age, but in any age still to come."

Paul says,

The fruit of the revelation of the knowledge of God will bring <u>to your understanding</u>

"...***the immeasurable greatness of His power <u>in us</u>;***"

"...who BELIEVE according to the working of His power and of His great might;"

He says,

"...according to the working of His great might..."

Let's go back to Ephesians 3:7 for just a moment. Paul says,

"Of this gospel I was made a minister..."

Now would you agree with me that Paul's ministry was *effective*? Would you agree that it was *successful*? Would you agree that it was *anointed*?

I have a passion in my heart for every one of us to have a ministry like Paul's ministry. I believe it's available to every believer! I believe that the same school, the same Spirit school, the same apostolic school that educated Paul's spirit, is still available to every believer today, to equip us to become ministers; <u>to make us</u> ministers, effective and efficient ministers!

"Of <u>this</u> gospel <u>I was made</u> a minister..."

Ephesians 3:7,

"Of <u>this</u> gospel I was made <u>a minister according to the gift of God's grace</u>..."

I believe that the same school that educated Paul's spirit is still available to every believer today, *to be made a minister,* **not after Man,** *not after Man's influence or persuasion,* **not after Man,** *but after the revelation of the true gospel of Jesus Christ!*

Paul says in Ephesians 3:7,

"Of <u>this</u> gospel <u>I was made</u> a minister, <u>according to the gift of God's grace</u>..."

We all need to go and study Romans Chapter Five thoroughly. We need to study in Romans 5 **the gift of God's grace!** We need to study it **until it so burns in our spirit that we cannot help but speak of the things we've seen and heard,** to the point that we too can say with Paul,

"...we too have believed, <u>and so we speak</u>!"

He says,

"Of <u>this</u> gospel <u>I was made</u> a minister according to the gift of God's grace <u>which was given me by the working of His power</u>..."

Not from my notebook, amen ...although I do encourage you to take notes and to read this book again and again until the revelation of what we are saying is burned into your spirit.

*Listen; I really want you to be aware of the fact that **it will never be yours until the working of His power is released in your inner man <u>through your focus upon the gospel</u>, and your heart begins to burn within you, it begins to burn with the conviction of God's truth and of God's love, and your heart is set ablaze with the conviction of the truth of His redemption!***

Paul says,

*"...**the gift of God's grace was given me, by the working of God's power**..."*

*"...**by the working of God's power**..."*

Back to Ephesians 1:19 now, where Paul says,

The fruit of the revelation of the knowledge of God, *will bring <u>to your understanding</u>,*

*"...**the immeasurable greatness of His power <u>in us</u> who BELIEVE**..."*

He says,

*"...this is **according to the working of His power and of His great might.**"*

Do you see, he is mentioning again and again,

*"...**the working of His power**..."*

He says,

The fruit of the revelation of the knowledge of God, will bring <u>to your understanding,</u>

"...the immeasurable greatness of His power <u>in us</u> who BELIEVE..."

"...the immeasurable greatness ...<u>in us</u>..."

Do you know why we have hidden our lamps *under a bushel?*

The word *"bushel"* is a measuring term used in the market place. It focuses on measuring something while doing business in the market place, *with a view to profit or gain.* Thus it is an economic term. It speaks of getting caught up in always having to measure something, always remaining focused on greed and on self-preservation. It can therefore be a very restrictive measuring term.

So, why have we hidden our lamps under a bushel?

We have hidden our lamps under a bushel because, through our restrictive religious concepts, our supposed *"Christian"* religious ideas and traditions, *we have been confined under that same religious measure!*

And so we have confined the revelation of revelations!

We have confined the greatest revelation that has ever come to this planet! We have confined *the true gospel of Jesus Christ!*

...And so we have confined the power of God!

That gospel is the very power of God! And it's become hidden to our communities and our societies as a whole, worldwide!

They can no longer pick up the wonder of that fragrance of Him, *because we have so watered it down, and so mixed it with all kinds of other influences.* **We have accommodated lies in our lives** *to deliberately limit, and build an encampment, a fence, around the light, to box in the light of the knowledge of God, this wonderful knowledge, the greatest of all knowledge!*

And God wants to break that restrictive limiting thing off of that lamp, because it only serves to obscure that lamp; *the light of that lamp!*

Chapter 8

God Wants out of the Box!

Stop limiting God! Take the limits off of God, *and let Him out of your box!*

Man's definitions aren't big enough!

Our conclusions have not been big enough!

Our confined containers, *our doctrines and our ministry models and our church systems cannot hold Him!*

God is not restricted by our definitions or our four walls! There is no mold that can contain Him *except His own!* **His Gospel is every bit as big and as powerful as He is!**

That power, the power of the gospel can therefore not be limited to our denominational and doctrinal dogmatic barriers!

The truth will come out, *it will be revealed, it cannot stay buried.* **The love and truth of God will break through and it will not stay hidden anymore. All nations together will see it,** *and the truth will set them free!*

Habakkuk 2:14,

"For the earth shall be filled with the knowledge of the glory of the Lord, as the waters cover the sea!"

Remember Gideon's army and *those earthen vessels.* When those earthen vessels were broken, *the light shone forth and the victory was theirs! And the enemy took to flight!*

God wants to break through every bushel, every restrictive measuring container *and every restrictive measure!* He wants to break through *every measure that wrongly measures the love of God and the truth of the gospel, and every measure that wrongly measures that dimension of His love and of His power that is working within us!*

We have for too long *misinterpreted* <u>His Gospel</u> *and misunderstood the correct, accurate measure of it, the largeness of that love and of that truth!*

We have for too long limited the power of the gospel and the power of His grace, and of His Spirit. *We have limited it to many small minded restrictive and dogmatic theological definitions and doctrines!* And we have written volumes of books *to try and define and explain the working of His power,* **but while we remain shortsighted and cannot see the largeness of the measure of the love of God and the accurate revelation of the gospel, we**

remain limited and restricted and constricted *in every way* *by these very same definitions and dogmatic doctrines* **we have come up with**.

Listen, I say again, we cannot afford to come to incomplete and inaccurate conclusions about the love of God and about the truth of the gospel, *because the working of God's power* <u>*can only be the product of the revelation*</u>*. It can only be a product of* <u>that revelation that comes to you as you intimately interact with God in the knowledge of Him</u>*, as you come into His presence and His Spirit illuminates your eyes* <u>*and you begin to see as He sees*</u>*, you begin to see the richness of His inheritance, you begin to see the hope of His calling upon your life,* <u>*and you come into full agreement with Him*</u>**.**

Chapter 9

God's Reference and Foundation to His power

Let's continue to read,

Ephesians 1:18,

*"…I pray that the eyes of your heart be enlightened, to know the hope to which He has called you, **and to know what the riches of His glorious inheritance in the saints are**…"*

*"…and to know **the immeasurable greatness of His power;**"*

*"…**in us who BELIEVE according to the working of His great might, which He worked in Christ, when He raised Him from the dead, and seated Him at His right hand in the heavenlies**… (in the unseen realm of spirit realities)."*

I want you to see that the power of God *has a reference; it **has a source, a point of reference**.* We can all relate to a lamp, or to this light shining in my office so I can see enough to write this book. *We can trace it to a source, the light has a reference. And I want you to know that **the working of God's power***

which equips saints has <u>one</u> reference ...and it's *not some* **theological school**, *it's not some historical background.*

Its reference is related to *the working of His great might,* <u>which He accomplished in Christ Jesus,</u> **when He raised Him from the dead, and when He also raised us up with Him in resurrection life**.

He raised us up with Him to newness of life!

If that revelation is not the reference of your ministry, **then your ministry has no substance,** and what you will be left with is, *having to rely upon the persuasive words of human wisdom and human doctrine.*

But God has something that is of stronger stuff and stronger persuasion. *It is called resurrection life!* **There is more persuasion in that,** *than in any doctrine of Man!*

And that resurrection life, t*he power of God that conquered death and defeated darkness,* <u>**is the very reference to that working of His great might**</u> **equipping saints for the work of the ministry.**

It's that resurrection life <u>revelation</u> *that liberates you from the chains of your past!* It's that resurrection life <u>revelation</u> *that takes away your grave clothes that carries the smell of death.*

It's that resurrection life <u>revelation</u> *that destroys the yoke of bondage through sin, so that we will no longer be enslaved and addicted to its demands!*

It's that resurrection life <u>revelation</u> *that introduces you to newness of life; the old things have <u>all</u> passed away in His death and <u>everything</u> has become new!*

There is a new portion of life that God has in mind for this world! It's for your mom and for your dad and your sister and brother, *and for your neighbor, and the nations right at your doorstep!*

There is a new measure of life available to all! It is measured by the portion of Scripture which talks about, *the fruit of the travail of His soul which satisfies Him!*

The resurrection of Jesus is the door *that introduces the power of God to your spirit,* and it works in your Spirit *mightily!*

Hallelujah!

I would not be a minister of Christ, a New Covenant minister if I were still seeking to establish you in any other kind of confidence of ministry, *but the confidence that comes through that revelation, which came to us as a gift from God, the revelation of the resurrection of us all in Christ!*

I preach that LIFE, that newness of life, which is hopefully **now beginning to come alive in your spirit** as well **through faith, through hearing and understanding and fully embracing this gospel!**

(It might help you to get a hold of, and study, my books on: "God's Love For You!" "God's Inheritance In You!" "Offspring of God!" "God's Eternal Purpose" "You Are Innocent!" and "Fully Persuaded" to understand this gospel I preach more fully!

While I'm at it, I also want to recommend a few of my other books to read, and study: "Reigning in Righteousness" "Resurrection Life Now" "Grace Exceedingly Sufficient" and "Zoe")

Chapter 10

Dare to Proclaim the Gospel!

Your knees might be knocking together when you knock on that stranger's door, or that person's door, *but now something of that confidence begins to come across* **from within your spirit.**

Paul says,

"I was with you in weakness and in trembling…"

I did not want to offend you or interrupt your privacy, *but His love was burning in my spirit.* It is called **the love of Christ.** There was **a compelling influence in my spirit, a particular specific persuasion. It was Love's own conclusion I came to in the gospel.** There is a necessity that was laid upon me **to declare and make known to you that** gospel. And the dogs may be barking, *but the demonstration of the Spirit, the demonstration of the love and the life of the spirit, was ready in my heart* **to be revealed; and to be introduced to you with such confidence <u>that this word will not return void</u>.**

This word is not empty human doctrine, **but it is the substance of the mind of Christ and the thoughts and the very heart of God.**

God's heart is revealed, there in that word, to produce through that word, *the fruit of the gospel; that fruit that would most certainly please Him.*

You see, that is the confidence platform that God wants to create in your spirit, *so that you can shine as a light* **in the midst** *of a crooked and perverse generation.*

I praise God that we as His Church are not called to go and hide in a cave somewhere, to hide our witness, or to go and build high walls around us and try and preserve our testimony. No, thank God, but He sends us forth into this world **to shine,** *because we have a much stronger* **reference** *than anything that might come against us in this world,* to try and stop us, or try and intimidate us, or to try and silence us and kill our voice. That light of God has a **reference.** That light, *of the glory of the knowledge of Jesus in our spirits,* has a **reference.**

2 Corinthians 4:6 says that, *"It is the God who said: 'Let light shine out of darkness ...it is that same God who shone into our hearts ...to give the light ...to give the understanding ...of the knowledge ...of the glory ...that very glory of God ...revealed in the face of Christ."*

That's our reference; that knowledge revealed, that truth revealed!

That's our foundation!

That knowledge revealed, that truth revealed is the foundation of our confidence!

And Paul says that if you miss that, ***you miss it all!*** If you miss that in your church fellowship and in your ministry, ***you miss it all!*** And you will never develop the confidence and the boldness needed to go and do the work of the ministry ...and even if you do, *your ministry will be **in your own zeal.** It will be **the product of your own making,** and it will be oh **so ineffective.*** It will be *coerced and fake.* It will not be *real ministry,* **genuine ministry.** *It will not be **the real thing, and it will not accomplish what God wants to accomplish in the hearts of your hearers**.*

Paul didn't want us to miss it; he didn't want us to miss this revelation, so he prays that God would grant us the spirit of wisdom and revelation in the knowledge of Him. He prays that the Spirit of God would grant an understanding in the heart of the believer to measure the power of God, which is immeasurable!

It's immeasurable by human standards. You could measure the strength of an atom, you could measure the power of a bomb and the strength of electric energy; you can measure the power of some engine and you can even measure the strength of a Man, of a natural man. You can measure the strength of his soul, of his inner person; *but the power of God is immeasurable.* **That strength that God imparts to our spirits is immeasurable.**

Paul wants us to measure the power of God available to us, within us, **and discover that it is indeed immeasurable!**

For too long we have tried to limit that measure, **that glory of God abiding within us,** *that resurrection LIFE,* through our minds and our intellect and our little doctrines!

...But *"Jerusalem shall be inhabited as villages **without walls** because of the multitude ...and **for** the multitude!"*

"Enlarge the place of your tent!"

You see, we all pitch our tent and live in our comfortable little dwelling places around us, but God says, *'That tent is too small for the work that I desire to do within you.'* That tent of religious persuasion is too small, *it limits God!* **It limits the activity of His grace within you!**

Get out of the boat, Peter! Come and measure,

*"...**the immeasurable greatness of His power at work within you who believe!**"*

Ephesians 1:19,

*"...to know **the immeasurable greatness of His power <u>in us</u> who BELIEVE.**"*

*"...**the immeasurable greatness of His power which He worked in Christ when He raised Him from the dead and made Him sit at His right hand in the heavenly realm;**"*

"...far above all rule, and authority, and power, and dominion;"

"...and above every name that is named, not only in this age, but also in all future generations;"

"...for He has put all things under His feet;"

It is impossible to make a study of Ephesians Chapter Six without the revelation given in Ephesians 1:17-23. Ephesians Six speaks of the armor of the saint. I mean, you can dress yourself with any armor. You know, I can put you in the fanciest equipment, the most modern armor, and send you off into war, *and you can still die, even wearing that armor.*

You see, **this revelation is <u>the substance</u>! Our position with Christ, in the heavenly places, in the bosom of the Father, <u>is the substance</u>!**

Ephesians 2:6 says that *I have been raised with Him and seated with Him* in heavenly places, in the spirit realm, in the bosom of my Father, in that realm of spirit reality, in that realm of His embrace, *in that realm of His love and of His eternal truth and of His Spirit's embrace;* **of His Spirit's indwelling.**

I have been seated in that realm of eternal truth; of reality, authority, and victory, *which comes to my spirit through revelation, and it enables me, it empowers me, it strengthens me,* **to take my position.** I am empowered to take my rightful place **and reign in life and be effective in ministry to others!**

Chapter 11

This Grace Was Given

Let's go back to Ephesians 3:7,

"Of this gospel I was made a minister, according to the gift of God's grace, which was given me by the working of His power…"

And we can think *'Well, Paul was such a wonderful saint, such a chosen and favored, special individual.'*

...And then we read verse 8,

"To me, though I am the very least of all the saints…"

You see, you need to stop putting Paul and others on such pedestals, *and you need to see yourself in God's plan.*

*"To me, though I am the very least of all the saints, **this grace was given**…"*

What God accomplished in Christ Jesus on Man's behalf, on my behalf and your behalf, makes the difference! **The grace of God makes the difference!**

*"…even though I am the very least of all the saints, **this grace was given me**,"*

Ephesians 4:7 says,

*"**BUT grace was given**, <u>to each of us</u>, according to the measure of Christ's gift..."*

Another translation says,

*"**But <u>to each and every one of us</u> grace was given;**"*

*"...**ACCORDING TO THE MEASURE OF THE GIFT OF CHRIST.**"*

You see, I want you to know Paul, Jesus, the Father, and the Holy Spirit of Truth who inspired the Scriptures to be written, *wants you to know that the equipping for the work of the ministry is not the work of Man.* **Do not limit the work God wants to do in you and through you,** *through His word, through the revelation of redemption realities,* by looking at me as a person from a human point of view, by thinking, *'Rudi is going to train me.'* Don't limit the work God wants to do in you, by thinking, *'The next man is going to train me, or this is going to train me, or that is going to train me.'* No, <u>**it's the working of His truth within you**</u>, **that's going to train you!**

It's the working of His Spirit of Truth within you; *it's the working of God, by His Spirit, within you, which trains you!*

The best any of us ministers can do is *to create an environment, to introduce you to an environment* **where the living seed can prosper in your life.**

The best any of us can manage is but an introduction into these things, and introduction to Him!

But really, ultimately, each one of us individually is responsible to maintain that environment ourselves ...and even in our gathering together also as believers, as the body of Christ, as a church fellowship, to maintain a positive environment of encouragement, enthusiasm, and faith, <u>so that the working of His grace can continue uninterrupted within our lives</u>!

Can you imagine the impact of the multiplication *of Paul's focus on the truth of God's gospel* in the Church today?

Can you imagine the impact of the multiplication *of Paul's ministry of that truth of the Gospel* in the Church today?

Can you just imagine that?

You know, so often we the Church could imagine and begin to think and reason and argue, you know, if perhaps possible, *'Could we persuade God to send Paul back to 2015?'* or *'God, could You perhaps send Jesus instead? It's gotten that desperate!'*

Hey listen, God wants us to get the revelation that, *"The word is near <u>you</u>! Even in <u>your</u> mouth and in <u>your</u> heart!"*

Let me say it again,

That truth of the gospel is near you!

In your heart!

In your mouth!

I want to challenge you in this book with the potential *that **GOD** has for your life!* I want to challenge you with *the potential that GOD sees within you!* I want to challenge you *to no longer compare yourselves by yourselves,* **to no longer measure by a wrong measure, but rather to let the true revelation of Jesus, the true revelation of redemption, be quickened and come alive in your spirit.**

Allow that 'KAVAH', that intertwining, and that 'SUNESI', that flowing together, that coming together as two streams, that melting together of minds and of thought and of life ...*allow it to come into your spirit as you 'KONONIA', as you fellowship intimately with God, communing with Him in the truth of His word, sitting under His teaching and instruction, and dwelling in His presence.*

As you live your life, or as you walk the streets, actively witnessing, **let it all be the fruit of**

that 'KAVAH', of genuine intimate relationship. Let it be the fruit of that intimate intertwining covenant love relationship with Him, of getting caught up in His love and truth and faith!

Thank you my precious Father!

Thank you Lord God!

We call You 'ABBA' Father; DADDY God, by the witness of the Spirit!

*We thank you for the conviction that we have in our hearts, that **we are indeed children of God.***

And if children, *then we are heirs of God Himself;*

…of Your fullness, of Your love and of Your nearness; ***of Your intimate presence!***

God, You are our inheritance and our exceedingly great reward, *and we treasure You Father God!*

Thank you that we are ***joint heirs with Jesus,*** *of this glorious inheritance,* ***which is YOU; of the same intimate grace of life <u>in intimate fellowship with You</u>!***

Thank you that You quicken within us, Lord, the desire *to fully appreciate every dimension of the eternal desire of Your heart, every* *dimension of Your grace gift in Christ **so that we can walk in its light and in its life!***

We will not deceive ourselves, oh God, we are diligent about this very thing, **we seek to count and estimate, and calculate THIS gospel,** *THIS revelation of the truth of Your Gospel, for its value, for what it's truly worth, for what it truly communicates to us!*

Father, we seek to count and calculate, **<u>and treasure</u>** **the revelation of Jesus Christ and His successful work of redemption!**

*We count it **of greater value and importance,** Father, than any other gospel ...than any other thing we can learn through the wisdom of this world!*

Father, we count Your gospel of greater value and importance than Man's gospel!

We thank you for equipping us in THIS Gospel; *Your Gospel!*

We thank you for equipping us *in the truth of it!*

And we thank you for producing in us a ministry of like precious faith and power to that of the apostles ...a ministry of grace and of righteousness and of pure truth and of pure love and of LIFE; Your 'ZOE' life, Your glorious eternal abundant life, Father God.

We thank you for equipping us to be ministers of that LIFE and joy and peace;

We thank you that You are equipping us to be New Testament ministers, having a New Covenant ministry of reconciliation.

Thank you that we have a New Testament ministry, no longer ministering from the oldness of the letter that kills, but ministering in the newness of the Spirit of life!

Thank you for the privilege of working with You, bringing forth that newness of life in people's spirits, Father God!

Thank you for Your grace!

Thank you for Your work of redemption!

Thank you for what You are doing in our spirits!

Thank you that You are working within us, both to will and to do of Your good pleasure, *through Your word and through Your Spirit of love!*

We so appreciate Your eternal truth and Your love for us, working within us, working Your zeal within us, **working Your precious ministry of love, within us, and through us, Father God!**

We so appreciate Your love and Your precious anointing!

What a treasure we have in You!

Amen!

In closing, I urge you to get yourself a copy of *"The Mirror Bible"* available online at www.Amazon.com, and several other book sellers.

If you want me or someone a part of our team to come to where you are, *anywhere in the world,* and give a talk, or teach you and some of your friends, *about the gospel message and these wonderful redemption realities,* simply contact us at www.LivingWordIntl.com, or you can always find me on Facebook.

If your life has changed as a result of reading this book, *please write to me and let me know.*

I would love to share your joy, *so that my joy in writing this book may be full.*

"That which was **from the beginning**,

which we have heard

(with our spiritual ears),

which we have seen

(with our spiritual eyes),

which we have looked upon

(beheld, focused our attention upon),

and which our hands have also handled

(which we have also experienced),

concerning the Word of life,

we declare to you,

that <u>you also</u> may have this fellowship <u>with us;</u>

and <u>truly our fellowship is with the Father</u>

and with His Son Jesus Christ.

And these things we write to you that your joy may be full."

~ 1 John 1:1-4

About the Author

Rudi & Carmen Louw together oversee: Living Word International.

They also travel and minister both locally and internationally.

Rudi was born and raised in the country of South Africa, while Carmen grew up in Cortland, New York.

They function in the ministry of reconciliation (2 Corinthians 5:18-21) and flow strongly with the Holy Spirit and His anointing to teach, preach, prophesy, heal, and whatever is needed to touch people's lives with the reality of God's love and power.

God has given them keen insight into what He has to say to mankind in the work of redemption, *concerning the revelation and restoration of humanity's true identity.*

Therefore they emphasize, THE GOSPEL, IN CHRIST REALITIES, the GRACE of God, the WORD OF RIGHTEOUSNESS, *and all such eternal truths essential to salvation and living the CHRIST-LIFE.*

They have been granted this wisdom and revelation into the knowledge of God, by the resurrected Spirit of Jesus Christ, *to establish and strengthen believers in the faith of God, and to activate them in ministering to others.*

Not only are people set free from the poison and bondage of sin, condemnation and all kinds of intimidation, (upheld, strengthened and reinforced by age old religious ideas, born out of ignorance) **but many are brought into a closer more intimate relationship with Father God, as Daddy,** through accurate teaching and unveiling of the gospel message, prophetic words, healings and miracles.

Rudi & Carmen are closely knitted together with many other effective Christians, church fellowships, and groups of believers, who share the same revelation and passion **to make the gospel fully known to others and thus to transform the world we live in with the love and power of God.**

www.ingramcontent.com/pod-product-compliance
Lightning Source LLC
Chambersburg PA
CBHW071141090426
42736CB00012B/2194